THE DERB

PORTV

Pilgrimage t

Fieldpath above Crowtrees Farm.

THE DERBYSHIRE PORTWAY
Pilgrimage to the Past

A Walking Guide

Stephen Bailey

Scarthin Books of Cromford
Derbyshire
2008

Published 2008
by Scarthin Books, Cromford, Derbyshire DE4 3QF

© Stephen Bailey 2008

www.scarthinbooks.com

e-mail: clare@scarthinbooks.com

Typesetting and layout by CJWT Solutions, St Helens, WA9 4TX

ISBN 10:   1-90044-613-8
ISBN 13:   9 781900 446136

Printed by Cambridge University Press

Author and publisher have taken pains to make this book accurate and safe and can accept no responsibility for accidents and injuries incurred whilst using it.

Contents

Introduction

Mam Tor is arguably the most famous summit in the Peak District, presented as one of the 'Seven Wonders of the Peak' in Cotton's pioneering guide of 1681. It is also the site of the largest prehistoric hillfort in Derbyshire, at a height of over 500 metres. The first time I walked there I had two surprises. Approaching from the south over Old Moor I had been expecting to see a breast-shaped hill, as this is supposed to be the origin of its distinctive name. In fact, due to its geological make-up, the hill has suffered from successive landslips, and so now is somewhat misshapen. The second was the number of people walking up the Tor, given that it was a weekday: several school parties had beaten me to it.

This was the final stage of a journey that had begun in Nottingham. The existence of an ancient route (or routes) from the Trent into the Pennines called the Portway has been widely accepted, and is discussed by numerous writers, such as Dodd and Dodd (1980), as an accepted fact. It is, however, a controversial topic, and it seems unlikely that there can ever be general agreement on it.

My concern was to research this route, both on the ground and on paper, to establish whether it really existed and how old it might be. Although the entire distance of about forty-eight miles could be covered by a fit hiker in two days, this book is the result of several years' reading and walking. As will become clear, it is a subject on which it is hard to reach definite conclusions, and my ideas have been steadily modified as my research has progressed. No doubt others will wish to add their comments on what is presented here.

Despite this, it seems likely that a prehistoric trackway existed from the Trent valley northwest into the Dark Peak, and probably further. This route appears to have been carefully devised to minimise valley crossings, thus allowing easier travelling. In addition, defensible encampments seem to have been created at regular intervals to provide overnight accommodation. The route was apparently 'signed' by a series of natural and man-made landmarks, such as Robin Hood's Stride. This track was probably used by the Romans, especially before they built their own road network, and was later named the 'Portway', possibly by the Saxons.

The Portway continued in use throughout the medieval period, when it was mentioned as a boundary in various land documents such as the charter of Dale Abbey:

> Grant from William de Grey son of Henry de Grey to the same, of 23 selions of land in Sandiacre, lying near Portweye ... (cited in Cockerton 1935a p.21).

It may have remained in use, in part at least, until the early eighteenth century, but by then two developments were leading to the erosion of such ancient routes. Enclosure, both private and parliamentary, had been steadily parcelling the land into smaller fields with mainly drystone wall boundaries. Secondly, turnpike roads were an upgrading of the existing road network, with some new sections added to reflect the changing patterns of population, and also the need to collect tolls. The development of large-scale quarrying, coal mining and railway building in the nineteenth century completed the process by which most of the Portway was reduced to a series of minor tracks and paths.

One feature of my reading was to discover how little is known of even major sites on the route such as Mam Tor or Fin Cop. Although these may be labelled 'Iron Age hillforts', it is remarkable that we know almost nothing of the people, not even their tribal name, who built and used such places, in many cases over periods of hundreds of years. Despite much archaeological work, there are huge gaps in our knowledge of their way of life and culture. However, it seems likely that our distant ancestors belonged to a mobile rather than a static society, which had an effective road system at its disposal.

When I finally reached the top of Mam Tor it was getting warm. I had passed a large group of teenagers sitting on the grass further down. Their teacher was telling them to get out their worksheets. Did they all understand the concept of erosion, she asked. The faint sounds of the geography lesson reached me as I sat on a rock, enjoying the wonderful views of the Edale and Hope valleys. At the same time, a constant stream of walkers was coming towards me from the opposite direction, Lose Hill. Although we may never establish the precise nature of the various periods of occupation of Mam Tor, it seems that after several millennia this place remains a centre of fascination for many people.

Using the book

This is intended to be both a history and a guide to walking the Portway. The first section looks at the origins of ancient roads, as well as their likely users. One particular group of travellers, pilgrims in the Christian period and earlier, is examined next. The discovery of the Derbyshire Portway is described in section three, and its history tentatively outlined. Finally, the main part of the book is taken up with a description of the route from Stapleford, near Nottingham, northwest to Mam Tor in Derbyshire (see main map in centre pages).

This section divides the route into ten stages, each of which discusses the features of that particular stage, as well as providing a practical guide for walkers, along with photos and maps. These show a feasible walking route, which may not always coincide with the most likely line of the Portway. Clearly, these stages can be tackled in any order and in either direction, though the most rewarding approach is to cover the whole length. In some cases (for example around Wirksworth), two alternative routes are given.

Most of the route is easy walking, although suitable clothing and footwear are obviously advisable. It is also worth carrying the relevant Ordnance Survey maps (Landranger sheets 129, 128, 119 and 110, or the larger scale Outdoor Leisure sheet 24 and Explorer sheet 260, which cover most of the route). Although a few lengths have to be walked on roads, these are mainly quiet lanes, and altogether this makes for an exhilarating journey with some spectacular views, a consequence of the Bronze Age preference for ridgeway travel.

Stapleford Cross.

Standing stone above Wirksworth.

9

Acknowledgements

All researchers into the Portway owe a great debt to R.W.P. Cockerton, whose articles first presented and described the route. A full list of these, which should be consulted by anyone needing a more detailed approach, is given in Appendix 1.

Cyril Spencer published his *Walking the Derbyshire Portway* in 1993, which, as far as I am aware, is the only book dealing specifically with the subject and contains much useful information.

Adrian Henstock, former County Archivist for Nottinghamshire, kindly agreed to read the text and has provided much valuable historical guidance.

The staff of the Local Studies Library in Matlock have been consistently helpful and knowledgeable.

Members of the Wirksworth Writers group have given me much support and encouragement in the preparation of the text.

Above all, my wife and daughter have been an enormous help to me in preparing this work, both practically in providing editing and taxi services, and in terms of encouragement and advice.

However, any inaccuracies or misjudgements in the text remain my responsibility. I would welcome information and comment from readers about anything discussed here.

Stephen Bailey
stephen.bailey@w3z.co.uk
May 2008

For the latest news and views on the Portway visit the website
www.derbyshireportway.co.uk

1.
Ancient roads and their users

Roads are one of the missing pieces in our jigsaw of the past. This is partly because archaeologists have tended to concentrate on places such as tumuli, hill forts and settlements, where excavation is more rewarding. But another reason is that roads are difficult to date, so that what appears to be an ancient green lane may have been created during the enclosures of the early nineteenth century, while a busy main road may overlie and so completely obliterate a Bronze Age track. The difficulty lies in isolating a stretch of road and establishing that it was first used four thousand years ago, despite having been trodden by every generation since. As a result of these factors, the importance of roads and travel in pre-Roman Britain tends to be underestimated.

It is generally assumed that the first tracks must have been made by animals, either on their seasonal migrations or locally, to a drinking place. These tracks would have been used by hunters pursuing their nomadic existence in the post-Ice Age landscape. At this time the forest cover was thick enough to make movement away from the tracks difficult, and it seems unlikely that these scattered groups would have been able or inclined to construct their own roads.

Around 5000-4000 BC there was a gradual change from hunter gathering to farming; the beginning of the Neolithic period. Forests began to be cleared for cereal cultivation and grazing, although the herdsmen in northern districts would have continued a semi-nomadic existence long after this, taking their flocks to higher pastures in the summer. Evidence from a site near Parwich suggests that the higher ground, being better drained with lighter soil, was cleared first:

> By the Bronze Age, Dimbleby concluded, the hilltops were open pastures where limited cereal cultivation was practised, but patches of woodland and scrub, much as today, grew nearby. Thus tracts of upland may have been exposed by the Later Mesolithic period, but the valleys were in all probability still thickly wooded (Hodges, 1991, p.65).

The first settlement sites would also have been on the higher ground, and so at this point roads might have been developed to link them together, in the sense that existing animal tracks could have been improved or connected. Clearly a prehistoric landscape of farms, moors, woods and ceremonial sites needed a network of roads for many of the same reasons that we do today, both for local and everyday traffic as well as long-distance travel.

It has long been thought that the earliest long-distance routes were ridgeways. A number of examples in southern Britain are regularly mentioned, such as the Icknield Way running northeast into East Anglia, or the Berkshire Ridgeway. Taylor (1979) has argued that such routes may not be prehistoric, and that the apparent clustering of prehistoric monuments along their course may be coincidental, for high land is less intensively farmed today and therefore features such as barrows tend to survive better. While it may be true that at some periods in prehistory the population density was high enough to require the clearance of lower, heavier soils, it still seems reasonable to assume that long-distance travel was mainly along upland routes.

There were several valid reasons for this preference for ridgeways. Not only was the higher ground less thickly wooded, but also by keeping to the heights travellers were saved the effort of climbing in and out of marshy valleys. In addition, navigation was made easier by enabling travellers to orientate themselves on distant landmarks. While there would clearly have to be river crossings in some places, where fords were established, the need for these was kept to a minimum.

Road users

It seems likely that from the beginning of agriculture, and hence settled populations, a wealth of short paths and lanes developed, known intimately to locals. But there must also have been a network of distinct long-distance tracks which could be used by travellers who did not know them well. The route of the Derbyshire Portway suggests that at some point a long-distance route through the Peak District was planned, since its line provides the easiest possible journey from the Trent to the Hope valley and beyond: it is not just a collection of disparate local tracks linked together.

We need to consider who were the travellers in Neolithic and Bronze Age Britain, and to do this the common assumption that pre-modern people did not travel widely must be challenged. Because long-distance travel is easy and frequent today, there is a tendency to assume that earlier generations were rooted to the spot. However, even in the historical period there is abundant evidence of ordinary people making long journeys on foot to seek work, for pilgrimage or to trade. Neolithic flint tools found at Roystone Grange (near Parwich), for example, were made from stone found in the Trent valley or the Lincolnshire Wolds (Hodges, 1991, p.60). Given that the earliest people were nomadic, it seems reasonable to assume that long journeys were often made in prehistoric times, and not only by specialists such as drovers.

Travellers in this period would have included the packhorsemen who made a living transporting scarce commodities such as salt and metal ores, and probably merchants carrying more exotic items imported from the continent. In addition, farmers had to move their livestock and produce to market, as well as herd animals to and from seasonal pasture. There would have been migrants seeking fresh opportunities in uncultivated areas, and possibly officials of the local chief or lord. Pilgrims had to travel to ritual sites (see section 2) for ceremonies connected with the progress of the year. Road use would presumably have been largely seasonal, since long-distance travel in winter must have been arduous.

Navigation

Anyone who has ever tried to find their way in unfamiliar countryside through a network of paths, sheep tracks and bridleways, even with the help of a good map, will sympathise with the problems early travellers would have faced in the same situation, but without the map. Taylor (1979) is dismissive of the difficulty: 'Indeed we do these prehistoric people a grave injustice in even conceiving that they needed such help to find their way across a country which must have been as familiar to them as our towns and village are to us' (Taylor, 1979, p.8).

But given that all roads were unsurfaced, the difficulty for strangers in distinguishing between a track to the nearest farmyard and the track to the Lake District must have been formidable. In a pre-literate society only two solutions could have been employed. Either travellers memorised a series of distinctive natural landmarks, which they used to orientate themselves, or else a series of man-made route markers, like waymarks on modern footpaths, were used to distinguish the 'highway'. These would most likely have been standing stones or piles of stones, supplemented at a later stage by stone crosses and later still by milestones. Hallenday (2001) describes a similar method (piles of stones) known as *Inuksuit* stone figures, used by Inuit people in the Arctic.

It is not clear whether tumuli or barrows were located beside long-distance roads, as Roman burials certainly were. A considerable number can still be found alongside the route of the Portway, though this may be coincidental. However, Bevan (2004), writing of a barrow in the upper Derwent valley, says:

> This barrow was designed to be seen by people moving across the landscape, maybe placed to identify traditional claims to hunting grounds or seasonal pastures…These were places which may have been shared pastures for surrounding settlements at lower altitudes.

In the last few hundred years the combination of enclosures and more intensive agriculture has led to the loss of many stone markers and barrows, as for example at Wardlow Mires, which makes it difficult to reach a conclusion on this issue.

Research difficulties

As mentioned previously, there are distinct problems with studying the history of roads. Many ancient routes which have remained popular are now covered by tarmac. On the other hand, once roads go out of use they are liable to disappear completely. Even Roman roads, which were generally engineered and surfaced, have not been fully mapped, so the difficulty of establishing routes which were mainly defined by wear and tear can be appreciated. The huge changes that can take place in a few hundred years can be seen from the example of the A6 between Belper, Cromford and Matlock. Today this road seems the natural route along the Derwent valley, and it is hard to imagine the situation in the early eighteenth century when there was no road there at all, until the demands of the mills at Belper and Cromford led to its creation.

Establishing a route three or four thousand years old will clearly be tentative. Maps are of limited use before the late eighteenth century, as roads were rarely

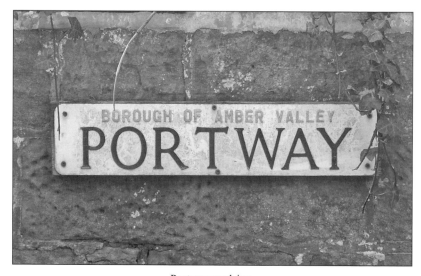

Portway roadsign.

14

shown with any accuracy. Place name evidence may be of value, but must be approached cautiously. It should be remembered that the very concept of a 'road' has changed over the millennia: prehistoric routes, which crossed mainly uncultivated ground, may well have spread over a mile or more in width, and instead of following one closely defined path they would have consisted of several interlinked tracks, so that if one became impassable a parallel track could be used. Only when agriculture became more dominant would roads have been gradually narrowed.

Despite these considerations, ancient societies can no more be understood without an appreciation of their road systems than could our own. Mobility was not a luxury in prehistoric Britain, it was essential to both the survival and development of the people, who only made the transition from a nomadic life to a more settled mode a few thousand years ago.

2.
The tradition of pilgrimage

Pilgrimage in British history has usually been treated as a medieval phenomenon, and little attention has been paid to its likely role in pre-Roman Britain. Yet given that it was being practised in the third millennium BC in Sumeria, and in the second millennium among the Hittites of Anatolia, and was certainly widespread in Classical times (Elsner & Rutherford, 2005), there is no reason why it could not have been a feature of pagan religion in Britain. A pilgrimage tradition has been found in most societies around the world, including Australian aborigines, New Zealand Maoris and the Zuni Indians of southwest USA. Indeed, it can be argued that the crowds who filed past Lenin's tomb in Red Square or the cultural pilgrims who flock to 'Brontë country' are obeying the same basic impulse.

Pilgrimage, usually meaning a sacred journey to a shrine, often the burial place of a holy person, is a feature of all major world religions. By making this journey pilgrims may feel they are approaching the divine, in the shape of the saint who became semi-divine. In some cases it is a group activity linked to a specific festival, such as the Islamic Haj to Mecca or the Hindu festival of Kumbla Mela; in other cases it is performed as an individual act of penance or to request divine intercession for an illness. In most cases some discomfort and effort seem to be required, and a distinction is emphasised between everyday existence and the special conditions of the journey.

Preston (1992) states that pilgrims' destinations tend to be situated in striking places: 'pilgrimage sites are often found in the most dramatic locations on the globe and inspire lofty emotions and high spiritual values' (p.35). He notes that many are on mountain tops, islands, or near lakes and rivers, and are frequently difficult to reach, which may make them more attractive. In some cases pilgrims make their journeys more demanding by imposing arduous conditions on themselves, for example crawling on their knees.

Clearly pilgrimage was a feature of Christian life in Britain, as in the rest of Europe, from the early church to the suppression of the monasteries in the sixteenth century. What is often regarded as the foundation of English literature, Geoffrey Chaucer's *The Canterbury Tales*, portrays the diversity of pilgrims in the medieval period, and historians have emphasised the wide social spectrum of pilgrims attending both local and national shrines. The extent to which the concept of pilgrimage was part of the national psyche is shown by the success of John Bunyan's *Pilgrim's Progress*, published in 1678, which quickly became a best seller, despite pilgrimage having by then been effectively abolished for over a hundred years.

In the Middle Ages churches and monasteries competed for the offerings made by both rich and poor pilgrims, leading them to struggle to acquire the most impressive relics for miracle working, in some cases using armed robbery. This indicates the economic importance of the tradition, reinforced by the fact that pilgrimage provided a welcome break from mundane daily toil. This 'holiday' aspect may have been a factor in the ending of the practice, as Protestantism gathered strength and scepticism about miracles increased in the sixteenth century.

Morley Cross.

But it can be argued that the tradition was carried on by the invalids who went to 'take the waters' at spas such as Buxton and Matlock which sprang up in the eighteenth century. There are other aspects of modern tourism which are reminiscent of pilgrimage, for instance attendance at famous 'shrines' such as the Eiffel Tower or Buckingham Palace (Cohen, 1992).

In Derbyshire it seems probable that the Portway was used by medieval pilgrims visiting Dale Abbey, where relics associated with St Mary were kept. The ancient church at Wirksworth, also dedicated to St Mary, may well have attracted pilgrims, as might the other churches on the route at Sandiacre, Morley and Ashford. It must be remembered that pilgrimage did not always involve a long journey; for poorer people a day's trip to a nearby church might have been all they could afford.

It is more difficult to identify likely destinations for pagan pilgrimage, but Mam Tor seems a likely ritual site for Bronze Age society, while Fin Cop also has a remarkable situation. Although we can never confirm this hypothesis, it should be remembered that one kind of pilgrimage is still popular in Derbyshire today, namely visiting well-dressings during the spring and summer. Although largely a modern (and Christianised) revival, there seems little doubt that well-dressing was an ancient practice which may have been linked to an early summer festival. Most pagan religions in agricultural societies have been concerned with ensuring crop fertility and the regularity of the seasons, and it would be surprising if the early farmers of the Peak did not have similar concerns.

3.
The Derbyshire Portway

The possibility of a prehistoric trackway running through Derbyshire and called the Portway was first proposed by the eminent local historian R.W.P. Cockerton (1904-80). A Bakewell solicitor, he was an expert on the Roman period in Derbyshire, being involved in many excavations. He published a series of articles in the *Derbyshire Countryside* between 1932 and 1936 (see Appendix 1) which set out his thesis. His starting point was the existence of a string of 'port' place names, such as Alport and Alport Height, which mark a line running from the northwest to the southeast across the county. On the ground these seem to be linked by a credible route, although there are sections where this is unclear. Secondly, there is reference in medieval documents such as charters to a 'Portawaye', often used to define land boundaries. Finally, he pointed to the physical existence of tracks and paths, which in many places were unrelated to local needs and historical settlement patterns (e.g. Dudwood Lane, which runs between the villages of Elton and Winster, without linking them).

There are a number of portways in England, such as the route from Silchester to Salisbury, but there is no agreement about the meaning of the name. Cockerton devoted two articles to the subject without reaching any definite conclusion, and the simplest explanation seems to be that it either meant something like 'main road', or was actually a road to a port. It must be emphasised that the word 'portway' is Anglo-Saxon, and although this name is crucial, his thesis was that the route was prehistoric in origin. It is likely that the Saxons were naming a pre-existing routeway, and recognising that such routes were a significant landscape feature. It should be noted that the earliest documentary evidence of the name is from the thirteenth century.

Another possible meaning of 'port' discussed by Cockerton was the idea of sanctuary or shelter, as a seaport is a haven for ships. In this sense a portway could have been a route with shelters at intervals of a day's travel. There is a case to be made for this theory in relation to the incidence of fortified sites along the route e.g. Fin Cop and Harborough Rocks. Clearly, a major problem for long-distance travellers was where to spend the night. Not only food and shelter, but also protection from wild animals and possibly robbers was required. In an age before inns, a defensive site where travellers could cook and sleep safely would have made long journeys feasible.

Cockerton had a formidable knowledge of the history of Derbyshire roads, and his articles deal with each section of the Portway, from the north around Wardlow to the Derbyshire border at Sandiacre. Subsequent historians of Peak

District roads such as Dodd and Dodd (1980) have accepted Cockerton's thesis without attempting to establish the Portway's purpose or likely route beyond the county. In any case, such discussion is highly speculative, since all road systems evolve continually to meet changing needs.

The economic life of the Peak District, for example, has fluctuated significantly with the climatic and other changes of the last six thousand years, with marked periods of recession and depopulation. At different times the

Guidestone at top of Crowhill Lane.

Portway might have carried lead ore from the mines near Wirksworth, groups of migrants or invaders, and pagan or Christian pilgrims. All would be using it as a convenient route from the river systems of eastern England into the northwest.

Nottingham was for many centuries the head of navigation on the Trent; a bridge was recorded there as early as 924 AD (Stone, 2005), and this would have been the usual upper limit for sea-going vessels. Therefore a possible destination for the Portway could have been the port of Nottingham, and it can be traced as far as Stapleford, only five miles from the modern Trent Bridge. In the other direction the road may well have crossed the Pennines into the northwest, but this present study will focus on the section from Nottinghamshire to Mam Tor.

It is impossible to specify the date when the Portway would have come into use, but it may be linked to the remarkable growth of population which occurred in the Peak District between 2000-1000 BC. According to Hodges (1991), this happened as a result of a period of climate warming which led to summers being 2-3° C warmer than they are now. Remarkably, it has been estimated that parts of the area had a population similar to that of today. This was the period when Arbor Low was first constructed, and which has left a rich archaeological legacy. Presumably both cereal cultivation and pasture for cattle were expanded to support the increase in numbers. But as cooling set in before 1000 BC a process of depopulation began, especially on the East Moors. Elsewhere (e.g. Mam Tor) the construction of defensive earthworks is suggestive of growing insecurity, presumably as a result of shrinking food resources. There is a noticeable scarcity of Iron Age finds in the Peak District, which historians have explained by the abandonment of marginal land.

The Portway probably enabled the Romans to gain access to the region before they constructed their own road network. Their arrival certainly brought about a period of economic growth, both in terms of providing a market for agricultural produce and the development of mining, especially for lead. It seems likely that the Portway was used by the Saxons, and there is archaeological and written evidence of medieval and later use. Features such as the hermitages seem to have been in use in the thirteenth and fourteenth centuries, while in the early eighteenth century sections were still used as a route from Derby to Manchester.

But in the seventeenth and early eighteenth century significant changes began to alter the Derbyshire landscape and led to the demise of the old road as a long-distance route. Enclosures, both private and parliamentary, brought about the end of the medieval system of open fields and common grazing on the moors, and caused the construction of the dense grid of dry-stone walls that now seems so characteristic of the area. (Some walls are much older, but the majority date to these enclosures.) At the same time turnpike roads were constructed to speed up travel, and in order to maximise toll collection some older routes were closed to prevent traffic using them to avoid the toll bars. Crowhill Lane, near Ashford, is an example of this practice, being a replacement for the old route which would have by-passed the toll house.

Milestone on Castlegate.

Simultaneously, the demands of an industrialising society led to the growth of large-scale quarrying and the rapid expansion of lead and coal mining in the region, as well as the construction of railways. All of these developments combined to obscure and in places obliterate the old route, so that by the nineteenth century it was only used for local traffic, although remarkably its name survived in places, for example between Holbrook and Coxbench.

Over a period of several thousand years it cannot be expected that the exact line of the original route, if there ever was one, can be fully traced. There is also the possibility that there was more than one 'portway' in the county, for example a branch may have run northwest from Harborough Rocks towards Arbor Low and Buxton. Perhaps what is remarkable, given the huge time span involved, is that a considerable proportion of the route can still be followed on footpaths and green lanes. It may be that ultimately it is the walker who is best placed to judge the validity of this route as it was originally devised, to allow travellers on foot to pass through the Peak District as safely and speedily as possible.

4.
A walk on the Portway

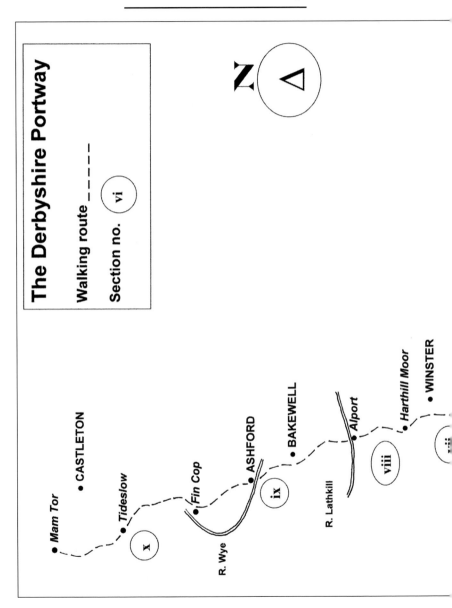

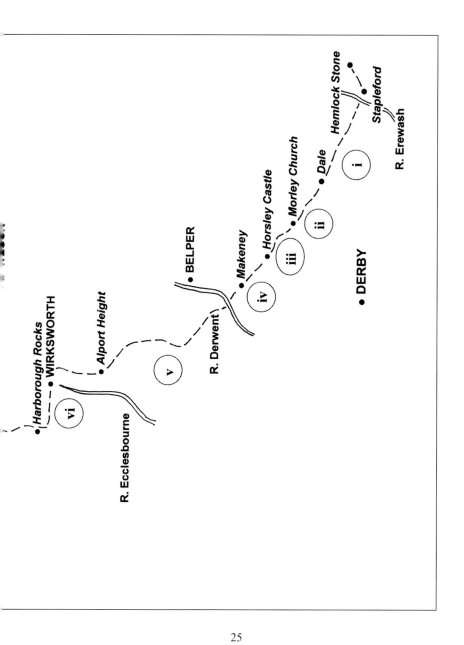

Harborough Rocks
WIRKSWORTH
Alport Height
R. Ecclesbourne
BELPER
R. Derwent
Makeney
Horsley Castle
Morley Church
Dale
Hemlock Stone
Stapleford
R. Erewash
DERBY

i
ii
iii
iv
v
vi

i.
From the Hemlock Stone into Derbyshire

The Hemlock Stone is an impressive, heavily weathered sandstone column, standing over six metres high near the top of Stapleford Hill. Although there are outcrops of sandstone all around Nottingham, this is quite different in terms of size and prominence. The bottom is reddish, but the top half is darker. There is no indication that it is anything but a natural feature yet, given the softness of the sandstone, it could have been cut or modified by human activity to create a marker.

Over the years there has been much inconclusive speculation about both its name and history. There are associations with the spring festival of Beltane, which was marked by the lighting of bonfires. According to Hutton (1996), the hill is one of the few places in England with documented evidence of the celebration of such May Day (or Beltane) festivities. These may have been linked to the stone, which could have acted as a route marker on the southern section of the Portway, given that it would be visible to travellers coming from the west towards the Erewash crossing a mile away. There is also the possibility that it was a boundary marker to advise travellers that they were entering a new tribal territory, 'hem' meaning edge or border.

In establishing the line of the Portway on the boundary between Nottinghamshire and Derbyshire the crucial factor is the river crossing. Although the Erewash (the 'meandering stream') today is only a few yards wide, it must have been a much more serious obstacle before being confined within its present banks. The name Stapleford is Saxon, meaning 'ford marked by a post'. The present church dates from 1220 AD, but in the churchyard is an ancient cross, believed to have been carved before c.800 AD, which might have been the post (or steeple) from which the town derives its name. It is the oldest church monument in the county, and although now in the churchyard, it has had at least one other location, so it is unclear where it was originally sited. It is also noticeably un-cross-like, without arms, but covered in scrollwork and the upper part has four faces, much worn, one of which is said to represent St Luke. It could well have served both as a base for travelling preachers and as a marker for the ford. Over the road the Old Cross pub reinforces the significance of the monument, which probably greatly predates any other structure in the town.

By the Erewash, the Old Mill is today a rundown-looking working men's club, but it may be the same building as the watermill shown at this site on Sanderson's map of 1835, with a millpond to the north, no trace of which is visible now. What is significant is the line of the footpath route, which runs from here over the river and the water meadows, then via a long ugly bridge over the railway line and sidings, before crossing the Erewash Canal. Clearly, this path was important enough to keep open when the new modes of transport came along, suggesting long usage. From the canal bridge there is a spectacular view of Sandiacre church with Church Farm in front, high up on the Derbyshire side of the valley.

Standing in Sandiacre churchyard there is a clear view east towards the spires of Stapleford and Bramcote. This platform would have given travellers a good perspective of the next stage of the road. The church (St Giles) is peculiar in many ways. It is on the northern fringe of the modern town, which has developed to the south around the old Derby road, and is perched on a hilltop, with a Romanesque nave and a taller fourteenth-century chancel. Pevsner (1978) describes it as 'the most interesting in the neighbourhood' (p.312). Its prominent siting may be explained by its position on the line of the Portway, serving as a landmark and possibly as a shrine for pilgrimage.

Sandiacre from canal bridge.

Sandiacre is the first place on the route with a documentary reference to the 'Portweye'. Cockerton tells us that the name occurs several times in a thirteenth-century charter of Dale Abbey, the road acting as a boundary to various pieces of land, some of which can still be identified in the vicinity of the route (Cockerton, 1935a). On the Sanderson map of 1835 Stanton Road is called Ladycroft Lane. However, one of the last houses on the right before crossing the M1 motorway, which appears to date from the late nineteenth century, is called Ladycross Cottage. It seems clear that the road was actually Lady*cross* Lane, which suggests a roadside cross in this vicinity, perhaps marking the route to St Mary's (Our Lady's) Abbey at Dale. The 1896 OS map also shows a large house near here named Ladycross House.

The next stage of the route, beyond the Risley road, is called No Man's Lane, the meaning of which is unclear, though it may be an ironic reference to Ladycross Lane (i.e. lady = no man). An alternative suggestion by Cockerton (1935a) is that the road was not the responsibility of either bordering parish, so the name means 'unadopted'. It soon becomes obvious that this is a ridgeway with remarkable views, first over the Trent valley to the south and then into the

Looking east from Sandiacre church.

28

White Peak to the north. Crich Stand and Alport Height are visible on the horizon, as are Stapleford Hill and the Hemlock Stone looking back east, while the white sails of the Cat and Fiddle windmill make a distinctive landmark to the northwest.

When the road makes a sharp right turn Boyah Grange is straight in front, consisting of two large farmhouses set back from the road down a track. Cockerton (1935b) suggests that the original line of the Portway ran through Boyah. The field between the farmhouses and the road is full of bumps and hollows, and is called the Cunnery on old maps, suggesting the keeping of rabbits, but this does not explain the origin of the earthworks which encouraged the animals to burrow there. 'Grange' means a monastic farm, which is not surprising with an abbey only a mile away.

A Roman aisled hall was excavated between 1994 and 1997 a mile to the southwest at Hay Grange. The report (Palfreyman, 2001) shows that this area was in mixed cultivation by the late Iron Age before the Romans arrived, although the economic changes they brought about probably stimulated agricultural production. One interesting aspect of the dig was the large quantity of lead objects found; it appears that this metal was cheap at the time, possibly because the Romans were extracting silver from the lead ore and so needed to process large quantities, leading to a glut of lead.

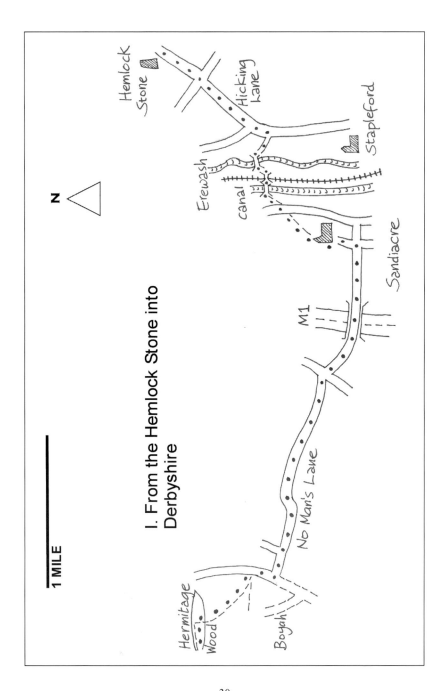

I. From the Hemlock Stone into Derbyshire

1 MILE

N

Hemlock Stone

Hicking Lane

Stapleford

Erewash

canal

Sandiacre

M1

No Man's Lane

Hermitage Wood

Boyah

The Hemlock Stone to Dale Hermitage – about 4½ miles

The Hemlock Stone is on Stapleford Hill, about five miles west of the centre of Nottingham. Access is from Coventry Lane (B6004), and there is free car parking in Bramcote Hills Park opposite (entrance on Ilkeston Road). From the park the route crosses Ilkeston Road and follows Hicking Lane, which continues in the same south-westerly direction into the centre of Stapleford. The lane, lined with mainly 1950s semi-detached houses, shows signs of having once been a rural route, as there are fragments of old hedges in places.

Crossing Church Street and turning left, the river Erewash can be reached via Manor Avenue or Mill Road on the right. These run through an area of Edwardian terraced houses, and lead to the Old Mill. Cross the river by the steel bridge and follow the track to the railway footbridge. Beyond this, take the stone bridge over the canal and then bear left over the meadows, which have clear ridge and furrow marks, to the Stanton Gate Road. This must be relatively recent, as it is not shown on the OS map of 1896. Go over this and then uphill across another pasture to join a well-defined old track, worn into the rock, which comes out by Sandiacre church.

Leave the churchyard on the south side and follow Church Drive downhill, turning right onto Stanton Road. After crossing the M1 the pavement gives out and it is road walking until Dale. The busy Stanton-Risley road is crossed, and then the road climbs past a large house on the right called The Hewarths. 'Heworth' is a name mentioned in the thirteenth-century charter. This stretch is called No Man's Lane both on the map and on roadside signs.

After going steadily northwest for about a mile the road swings sharply right and widens out at a pair of Victorian cottages. It is then downhill walking to the right- angle bend at Boyah Grange. Turn right here before coming to a footpath on the left. Take this, but instead of following it to the farm head northwest, skirting the hollow, and join the footpath running in the same direction across arable land. This leads to Hermit's Wood, a narrow belt of woodland on the scarp face. Various steep paths drop down through the wood, and the hermitage can be found in the cliff face.

ii.
Dale to Morley

The field path from Boyah to Dale is in alignment with the last part of No Man's Lane, and presumably the Portway would have dropped down into Dale on the grass slope between the two sections of rocky outcrops, to the west of the present footpath. The hermitage, cut into the cliff face, seems improbably open for year-round occupation, but possibly a wooden framework, let into the cliff face, would have given more protection and space. This is a lovely spot, with good views over the valley through the trees, which might have compensated for the drawbacks of cave life.

The legend of the foundation of the abbey begins with the story of a devout Derby baker who was told in a dream by St Mary to abandon his home and go to live in Depedale. It is claimed that he excavated the hermit's cave on the south side of the valley in the first half of the twelfth century, and his holy influence led to several attempts to establish monastic life in the area, which were finally successful with the arrival of the Premonstratensian Order in about 1200.

A history of Dale stresses the wild and isolated nature of the district:

> We know nothing of Dale, or as it was anciently called, Depedale, previous to this period (the twelfth century), beyond that it was a marshy and lonely place in the midst of an expanse of woodland from Derby to the Erewash, unbroken except for a few scattered villages (Ward, 1891).

In fact by this period neither hermits nor monks were necessarily associated with wilderness. As Ward points out (of hermits):

> Their substantial little houses were usually placed where they could be of some service to their fellow men, especially to travellers, as by a bridge, a ford, a marsh, or at the meeting of ways in some dense forest … (Ward, 1891).

Dreams of prophetic instruction are a common feature of medieval religious culture, and it seems far more likely that the baker from Derby actually chose to live close to the line of the Portway, where the cliff face provided shelter and where guidance to travellers might have been needed on the steep incline. The old road between Derby and Nottingham may also have run through Depedale.

Later in the century the monks might also have seen the advantage of a site on an ancient line of communication, since they were becoming less concerned with sacred solitude than with encouraging pilgrimage and the income to be gained from it. Dale may not have been in the same league for pilgrims as Canterbury or Walsingham, but at the time of the Dissolution of the Monasteries in 1539 it is recorded as possessing relics associated with its patron St Mary, such as a girdle and some milk. It would have been a day's journey from either Derby or Nottingham: an ideal short pilgrimage for those needing the kind of cure or miracle St Mary might provide.

Today Dale is a distinctly up-market village, which has come a long way from the habitation of lowly monks and hermits. But despite this, it still has an air of seclusion, protected on the south by the sandstone scarp. The surviving arch of the east window of the Abbey Church gives an idea of the scale of the monastery buildings, but it is one of the few traces of the original structure to remain. Apparently it was preserved because of a belief that the village would be exempt from tithes as long as the arch survived, but the rest of the stone was removed to build (among other places) Risley Hall.

The most interesting building in Dale now is All Saints church, which was possibly once part of the abbey, but more likely the chapel of Depedale. Pevsner (1978) calls it 'one of the smallest and oddest of English churches' (p.163), not only on account of its size but because it is attached to a house on its west side, making it a very unusual semi-detached church. Inside it is only about eight metres square, and feels very crowded with box pews. Among its treasures are some fragments of thirteenth-century wall paintings.

The name of Arbour Hill, which dominates the road out of Dale, may be derived from the Celtic word *arrhber*, a fortress, according to Ward (1891). If this was a pre-Roman encampment it might well be linked to the Portway, which probably followed the line of the existing road. It is significant that there is a series of hilltop strongholds along the line of the Portway, one of which, Harborough Rocks (west of Wirksworth) has a similar name. These may have been fortified campsites established for the benefit of travellers, rather than castles in the medieval sense. This would mean that they were not created to dominate or control the road, as has been suggested, but rather to shelter road users.

In the section from Upper Hagg Farm to Morley the line of the Portway has been obscured by the building of the railway between Derby and Nottingham, and the development of Stanley Kilbourne Colliery. From Upper Hagg the most likely route is the track running west downhill towards Lower Hagg, which soon descends to quite boggy ground where 'coal pits' are marked on Sanderson's map and which were still marked as Kilbourne Colliery on the 1896 OS map. As it approaches the Stanley road the path becomes a track and then is called Dale Road, but 100 years ago was named Sough Lane. This may have been connected with the need to dewater the colliery. The Bridge Inn used to mark the junction, but this has now been converted into a private house, with only the signboard remaining as a reminder of the former inn.

This section of the Portway from Upper Hagg to near Morley is unusual in that it follows a stream and crosses low lying ground, which must have been swampy in winter. However, the only alternative is the lane going north from Upper Hagg Farm, which despite appearing to be an ancient sunken track, actually travels in the wrong direction, finishing on Cat and Fiddle Lane where it is then necessary to make a right- angle turn to the west to reach Stanley. This route also involves crossing marshy ground.

The most convincing evidence for the direct route is provided by the section between the railway embankment and Church Lane, Morley. The line of the old road is marked by a series of mature oak and ash trees, while in the section nearest to Morley there is a pronounced raised roadbed. The maps of 1835 and

Dale Hermitage.

34

1896 both show this section as a wide lane, which presumably went out of use when it was blocked to wheeled vehicles by the embankment's construction. The alternative route, which crossed the railway on a bridge, would then have replaced the original track. Both routes come together below Morley church. This final section of the lane is particularly attractive, with a vigorous stream running beside the road on the left.

Dale to Morley church – about 3½ miles

Follow the main track at the base of the cliff west to the church, and then turn north by the churchyard and go through the gate, which leads into the village street. This bends to the right, and at the end of the street turn left at the Carpenter's Arms to leave the village by the steep Arbour Hill. If preferred, road walking can be avoided by taking a path out of the village street parallel to the road, which runs to the south-west of the wooded summit of the hill.

At the top of Arbour Hill is the Spondon-Ilkeston road. Cross this and continue on the asphalt lane (Hagg Lane) to Upper Hagg Farm. Here the routes diverge:

a)   *The most direct route goes west past Lower Hagg Farm and emerges on the Stanley road by the old Bridge Inn. On the west side of the road the path continues beside the brook, then branches away to the west to cross the disused railway embankment. Beyond this it is marked by a line of oak and ash trees before joining Church Lane about half a mile below Morley church.*

b)   *The alternative route, north from Upper Hagg, possibly offers a better walk. Go straight on down the green lane until the old mill cottage is visible. This is shown as Baldock Mill on the 1896 map. Fork left here at the remains of a dam, which was probably built for the millpond. The path to Stanley now runs westward along the embankment or causeway between the fields above and the marshy ground below, a section which can be quite boggy in winter. The path runs into the centre of Stanley, emerging between the school and the church (St Andrew, mainly nineteenth-century rebuilding, but with some medieval fragments). Turn right at the White Hart pub from where Morley Lane leads north, then turn north east (Station Road) before crossing the now defunct railway. At this point the road turns into a track which runs downhill to a narrow ford and then climbs towards Morley, with the tall church spire acting as a landmark for much of the way.*

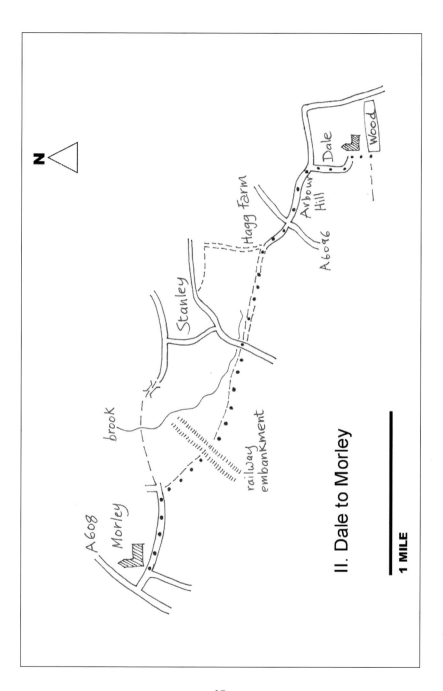

N

II. Dale to Morley

1 MILE

iii.
Ryknild Street & Horsley Castle

Morley churchyard is a peaceful place with a mausoleum and two crosses as well as the rectory, a tithe barn and the church itself. The latter contains an important collection of stained glass from Dale Abbey, removed at the time of the Dissolution. The south porch is also believed to have come from the same source. Pevsner (1978) says of the glass: 'enough remains to make Morley the most rewarding place in the country to study late medieval stained glass' (p.283). One cross, the Butter Cross, has an ancient stepped base with a modern (early twentieth-century) carved shaft, and is located on what used to be a village green. The other is shortened, with a sundial placed on top. Although the church is dedicated to St Matthew it may be significant that the patron saint of the Lords of Morley was St Christopher, associated with travellers.

One striking feature of the church is the height of the spire, which may have served as a useful landmark for travellers on this relatively flat section of the Portway. The wealth displayed in the church contrasts with the small size and dispersed nature of the modern village. But it had a strategic position at the junction of two major ancient routes; the Portway and Ryknild Street, an important Roman road which ran from Doncaster to the Cotswolds. The position of Breadsall Priory (now a hotel) a mile west of the church may also be significant, since good transport links would have been important to the Austin canons who founded it in the thirteenth century.

From Morley to Coxbench the route of the Portway is again problematic, but the first section is likely to have run towards Morleymoor. Just beyond the farmyard the track makes a sharp bend to skirt round an obstacle which, in summer, is almost invisible under its tree cover. Known as the Mound, this semi-moated site contains a man-made hill about six metres high, which appears to be sited on the exact line of the Portway. Apparently not a barrow, there is no agreement on the function or age of the Mound, which is clearly too small to be defensive. One theory is that it was a survey point for constructing the nearby Ryknild Street. It is interesting to note that near here there is a significant change of direction in Ryknild Street, from northeast to nearly due north, and the mound is in alignment with the northern stretch. Alternatively, it has been suggested that before the church was built the Mound was a lookout post, and given its position near the junction of two important routes, this hypothesis might have some validity. Or it could simply have been a route marker, fulfilling the same function in prehistoric times as the church spire did in the Middle Ages.

From Morleymoor the direct route northwest to Coxbench involves dropping into the steep valley of the Carr Brook. Although this direction can be followed on footpaths and tracks, it seems more likely that the ancient route turned to the north to stay on higher ground. It is also possible that after Ryknild Street was constructed, travellers used that route from Morleymoor to Brackley Gate and there turned west.

The road junction at Horsley Farm Park is an interesting example of the changes that can occur in the road pattern over a relatively short period. The present surfaced road (Sandy Lane) running down towards Horsley only dates from 1865, when the old lane to the left was blocked by the growth of quarrying. This was known as Park Lane, Horsley Park being the wide area to the north and south of Horsley Castle, originally a hunting ground for the landowner. This beautiful track is, in part, a ridgeway, and has views far to the north, with Alport Height again visible on the horizon.

Today almost nothing remains of the castle, which was apparently built in the eleventh century. The whole site is thickly wooded and full of hummocks, though it is possible to see fragments of a few masonry walls. One story is that the stone was removed in the eighteenth century to build Kedleston Hall, though this may refer to stone taken from the nearby quarry. As is often the case, there is little surviving evidence about the form or use of the castle. One explanation for the fortification of this site may be that the Portway was still an important route at that time. The medieval castle could have been built on the site of a prehistoric stronghold, possibly another encampment for long-distance travellers.

Evidence for this section of the route being pre-medieval is provided by the finding by two quarrymen of a Roman coin dating from 103 AD with some pottery fragments (Cockerton, 1936a). Another curious aspect of this locality is that the castle area used to be famous for its display of daffodils, and what is now a deserted wood was then something of a tourist attraction, with the farm offering teas.

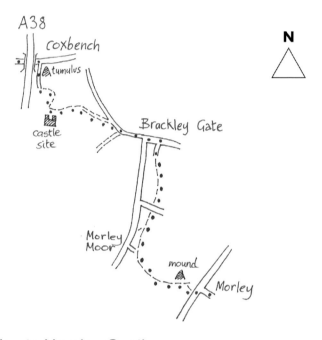

III. Morley to Horsley Castle

1 MILE

Morley to Coxbench – about 3¼ miles

Follow Lime Lane from the church to the main road (A608), cross this and pick up a track running northwest, starting at the farmyard of Morley House Farm. Beyond the Mound the track continues into Morleymoor, further suggestion of its age being the thick belt of holly and oak to the left, which may even be part of the original overgrown roadway. The Sacheverell Almshouses of 1656 are the most interesting feature of this part of the village.

At Morleymoor the best walking route is to turn north on a track just before entering the village. This runs beside an area of lake and wet woodland on the left, and is roughly parallel to the old Ryknild Street. After crossing Brick Kiln Lane it goes past Morleymoor Farm, an attractive redbrick house with deep sash windows, to emerge on the road at Brackley Gate . The route then turns west to Brackley Gate Farm, after which the road drops, but still has good views to the north towards Horsley. Take the unmade road on the left to Horsley Park Farm, which, remarkably, is well-stocked with horses.

The site of Horsley Castle is on the left in Castle Wood, obscured by the covering of trees. Beyond the castle the line of the original route is blocked by a chain link fence protecting a quarried area, which has clearly obliterated what may have been a direct route to Holbrook. The path now turns right to skirt this old quarry and descends to the A38 flyover at Coxbench beside the kennels.

Morley Mound.

iv.
Coxbench to Makeney

The presence of the A38, noisy on its embankment as it passes through Coxbench, makes it hard to imagine this valley when the Portway was the main route. The OS map of 1896 makes it clear how dramatically the landscape here has been affected by industrialisation. Before the modern road there was both a tramway and a railway, the latter with a spur into Coxbench quarry, which must have provided the main employment here.

To the east of the track, beside the brook and before reaching the village, is a tree-covered mound, not moated like the one at Morley, which seems man-made. According to Davies' *History of Derbyshire* (1811) it is: '...a large circular mound rising to a considerable elevation which appears to be an ancient tumulus. The old people call it "The Devil's Shovel-ful".' Because of its closeness to the new road, and the tree covering, the mound is no longer as prominent as it once must have been, but its proximity to the Portway may be significant.

Nearly underneath the flyover is the stone canopy of St Anthony's Well, with a notice saying that it had been moved from an (unspecified) cottage garden. According to Howe (1984), Coxbench was previously known as St Anthony's Cross, which may have marked the junction of the Portway with another route running up the valley of the Bottle Brook. St Anthony was noted for being an early hermit and ascetic. Why he should be connected with this spot is unclear, unless there was a hermitage nearby.

The next section of road, leading uphill to the village of Holbrook, is unique as it is actually called 'Portway' on OS maps as well as on roadside signs, a remarkable survival and the only section of the entire route to be thus marked. Despite this, tracing the route from Holbrook to the Derwent crossing is difficult. It may well have gone through what are now the grounds of Holbrook Hall, since when this was built in the mid-seventeenth century there was possibly a re-arrangement in the local road pattern.

What is surely significant is the discovery in the hall grounds, in 1962, of several pottery kilns dated to 170 AD (Howe, 1984). Two have been excavated, and the main product seems to have been storage jars of the type used by the Romans to provide their troops with storage for basic rations. The second kiln is the largest found in Britain from this period, so it was clearly doing more than supplying local needs; pieces of this pottery have been found at Roman sites in northern Britain. The jars may have been transported on Ryknild Street, or possibly the Romans used the older Portway as a route north. It is worth noting that the modern Denby pottery is just two miles to the east.

Holbrook church only dates from 1841, replacing a chapel of 1761. Dedicated to St Michael, the arched east window and pedimented belfry are distinctive. Holbrook was part of the ancient parish of Duffield until 1863, but the new building probably reflected the growth of population caused by the rise of the local framework knitting industry.

From the fieldpath down to Makeney there are tremendous views northwards, including the Chevin in the foreground and Alport Height in the distance. Somewhere around Makeney there must have been a ford, though the river banks and their fringing meadows have changed so greatly over the past few thousand years as to make finding the precise location difficult. According to Cameron (1959), medieval Makeney was a more important settlement than Milford, possibly as a consequence of the Portway ford having been nearby. The 1896 OS map shows a suggestive length of causeway on the far side of the river, just north of Moscow Farm, which can still be seen near the edge of a field to the west of the A6, just past Milford House. This might have led to a ford opposite Makeney House, and is in approximate alignment with the field path above the Holly Bush pub. This inn, which claims to be one of the oldest in the county, appears to be right on the line of the Portway, and is one of two with this name on the route.

St Anthony's Well.

43

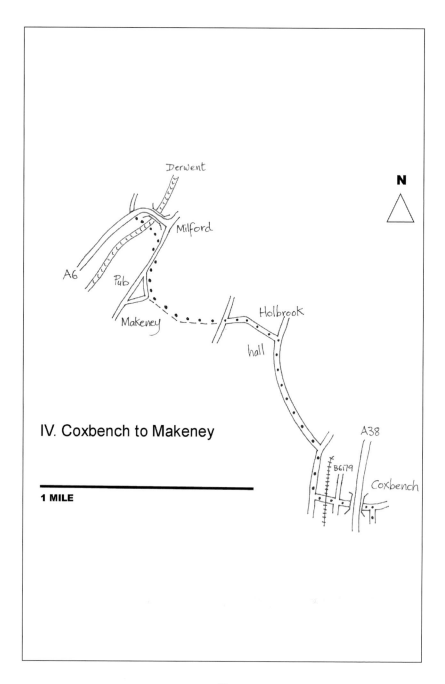

Derwent

Milford

A6

Pub

Makeney

Holbrook

hall

N

IV. Coxbench to Makeney

A38

B6179

Coxbench

1 MILE

Coxbench to Milford – about 2 miles

Turn left under the A38, cross the B679 and the level crossing and turn right past Coxbench Hall. Fork left after a few hundred yards. Continue uphill to Holbrook.

As the line of the Portway is obscure here, the best route through the village is to take Mellors Lane to the left and follow this past the playground to the junction with Makeney Road. A little to the left of this junction a field path can be found on the right which runs downhill to Makeney, to emerge by the steps above the Holly Bush pub.

Turn right at the pub and follow the road towards Milford. The simplest way to cross the Derwent is to take the pedestrian bridge at the garden centre, which gives excellent views of the weirs built for the now-demolished mill. This brings you out on the A6 by the Strutt Arms and opposite Chevin Road.

Steps above Holly Bush pub.

v.
Milford to Alport Height

Milford is a pretty village above the A6, with cottages of former millworkers banked up the slope. It is built at the southern end of the Chevin – a Celtic name meaning ridge – and this is the main landscape feature here on the west side of the Derwent, reaching a height of 190 metres. In this section the line of the Portway appears clear; it must have followed the crest of the Chevin northwards, along what is today North Lane. This is a wide, tree-lined track, with good views in places towards Belper on the far side of the Derwent. A railway tunnel on the Derby–Sheffield line runs under the Chevin near Milford, which explains the ruined tower at the village end, built to align the tunnel works which were engineered by Robert Stephenson. The first section of the lane is bounded by a golf course, and in the middle part is a massive stone wall on the right, about seven metres high and set at an angle to the track, which was apparently built as a shooting range in the nineteenth century.

From the junction with Farnah Green Road the original line of the way to Blackbrook is lost, but the alternative route is almost entirely on good footpaths. At Blackbrook Longwall Lane appears to resume the route of the Portway, climbing steadily and then steeply out of the hamlet. In places the floor of the track consists of large slabs of bedrock, which suggests erosion caused by heavy use. To the east of the lane, in the grounds of Starbuck House, a Romano-British quern manufacturing site has been recently discovered. These were small millstones about 35 cms across, essentially portable flour mills (Palfreyman & Ebbins, 2007). It seems likely that this site was chosen because the Portway offered convenient transport facilities for the finished querns, both north and south, presumably by packhorse.

Further on the lane levels out and offers good views on both sides. Looking back south beyond Blackbrook a belt of trees and the line of field boundaries running up the hillside must be close to the lost line of the Portway. In the other direction, towards the lane's end, Alport Height is clearly visible to the northwest, while there are several footpaths crossing the route. The wood on the east side has the suggestive name of Streets Wood, and the place where the lane joins Wilderbrook Lane is known as Knaves Cross (Spencer, 1993). The origin of this name is obscure, but it may have referred to a wayside cross, or even a gibbet.

Alport Height, a significant route marker, is now only two miles away, and a well-defined footpath runs almost straight across the fields, following the highest ground and offering wonderful views, especially south over the Trent valley. This is empty country, over 250 metres high, bleak enough even in summer, with swallows swooping over the grassland and a kestrel hovering near Crowtrees Farm. Compared with the other side of the Derwent there is a noticeable lack of villages on this plateau; in fact only hamlets are passed between Milford and Wirksworth.

The prominence of Alport Height (314 metres) is exaggerated now by the radio masts on the top, but even without these it would have been a useful landmark. However, it is worth noting that the stone pillar on the west face of the hill must have been created by quarrying and cannot be an ancient feature. Yet the name clearly links the hilltop to the Portway, and it has been sporadically visible since Sandiacre.

Longwall Lane.

Milford to Alport Height – about 6 miles

Follow Chevin Road to a road on the left called Sunny Hill, which climbs steeply to North Lane. This runs along the top of the Chevin for about a mile. At the far end the lane abruptly swings west and joins the road at Farnah Green. This diversion is shown on the map of 1835 and may have been caused by the building of Chevin Mount, the large house on this site. From here to Blackbrook (over half a mile) the line of the Portway is again unclear, but the best walking route is to turn briefly right into Farnah Green Road, then take a track to the left, but soon turning right along the top of the wooded Lumb Brook valley. After another right turn this track emerges at Blackbrook, only a hundred yards from the end of Longwall Lane (part of the Midshires Way).

Longwall Lane runs north for over a mile before reaching the junction of Knaves Cross. Turn left here downhill onto Wilderbrook Lane for a short distance and then take the path signed on the right. There should be no difficulty in following the track, as it is marked by a succession of squeeze stiles.

The last section, after crossing Palerow Lane, runs through muddy and unattractive pasture past Coneygreave Farm on the left and emerges at the crossroads of Peat Lane and Back Lane. Follow the latter to the east of the hilltop and the next road junction. The land on the summit (owned by the National Trust) can be reached by turning left from here.

View of Alport Height from Longwall Lane.

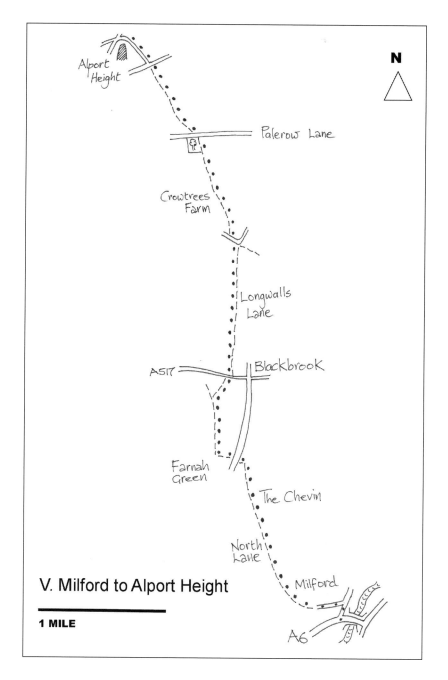

N

Alport
Height

Palerow Lane

Crowtrees
Farm

Longwalls
Lane

A517   Blackbrook

Farnah
Green

The Chevin

North
Lane

Milford

A6

V. Milford to Alport Height

1 MILE

vi.
Around Wirksworth

Less than two miles from Alport Height, Wirksworth is a characterful old town which sits at the head of the Ecclesbourne valley. This name may mean 'the stream of the church' (*egles* is Celtic for church), indicating the early importance of the town and suggesting that the church may have been founded in the Romano-British period. It has been claimed that Wirksworth was the centre of Roman lead production in the Peak District, the much-discussed lost town of Lutudarum. Whatever the truth of this, there is no doubt that lead was mined and processed here before, during and after the Roman period. The wealth generated by this industrial activity would have permitted church building at an early date. Much later, during the sixteenth century, Wirksworth was the second most important town in the county, an indication of the continuing value of its mineral riches.

Today the church of St Mary is still an impressive building, and it contains a remarkable carved coffin lid c. 650-800 AD, found below the altar in 1820, which may mark the burial place of an important Christian missionary or bishop. One legend links it to St Betti, an early Saxon missionary who died in the mid seventh century, but there are other candidates (see an exploration of this topic by Gladwyn Turbutt in the *Derbyshire Archaeological Journal*, 2007). The oval shape of the churchyard is said to be another indicator of the antiquity of the site. Clearly its position adjacent to the Portway would have allowed lead ore to be brought into the town, and then for pigs of lead to be transported either to a river for export, or via the road network to more local markets.

The Romans were certainly keen to increase lead production to satisfy their industrial needs, and a pig of lead was found north of the town in 1777 with a Latin inscription dating to the reign of Hadrian (Cockerton, 1936b). However, very little other evidence has been found from this period, and it may be that it was more of an industrial zone than a town. (A fuller discussion of Wirksworth in the Roman period is provided in Shone's *Origins and History of Wirksworth*.)

In its initial phase as a prehistoric trackway, the Portway would have avoided the low-lying site of the future town, and so would have looped around the valley to the east and the north. Possible support for this route is provided by the standing stone in the field opposite the Malt Shovel pub, and the name Porter Lane for the stretch of the B5035 between the Cromford and Middleton roads, which also serves as a parish boundary.

When Wirksworth became established, first as a mining area and later as a religious centre and market place, some travellers would have wanted to leave

Wirksworth Stone.

the old track and descend into the town. One likely route is via Prathall Lane to Gorseybank, then into the centre on the Derby Road. Leaving the town, the long climb up from the market place is marked by a standing stone above Norbreck Farm.

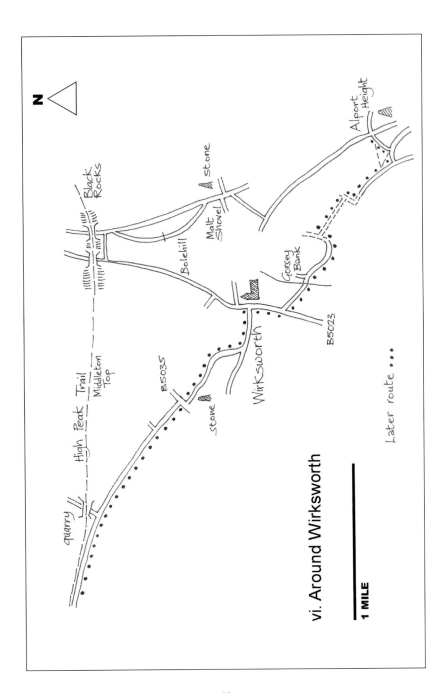

N

quarry

High Peak Trail

Middleton Top

Black Rocks

stone

Malt Shovel

Bolehill

B5035

stone

Gorsey Bank

Wirksworth

B5023

Alport Height

Later route ...

vi. Around Wirksworth

1 MILE

Ancient route – about 5 miles

From the crossroads near Alport Height take Alport Lane northwest, which becomes Hay Lane. Fork right into Breamfield Lane, which emerges near Moor Farm. Turn left, cross the Whatstandwell road and go past the Malt Shovel pub to the junction on the left with the lane down to Bolehill. This route has been closed to through traffic, which makes for more pleasant walking, but the original course of the Portway is more likely to have been on the contour line above. From Bolehill village walk up to Steeple Grange, where the building of the High Peak Railway clearly had a major impact on the landscape. The simplest and most pleasant route from here is to climb onto the High Peak trail at Black Rocks car park and follow it west past Middleton Top engine house to where it runs alongside the Brassington road.

Later route, through the town – about 4 miles

From the Alport Height crossroads go west downhill for half a mile. Take the path marked down the slope on the right, which joins Taylor's Lane and leads to Follywell Farm. From here a green though usually muddy track, Prathall Lane, leads to Gorseybank. Cross the railway and continue to the main B5023 Derby road. Take this into the centre of Wirksworth, with the secluded church and churchyard behind the shops on the right and the market place to the left. Turn left here up Westend and half a mile above the market the route forks right and continues on the fringe of an old quarry, past the ruins of several small field barns, to the crossroads with the Carsington road. Turn right and then shortly left, and follow the Brassington road west until it is possible to join the High Peak Trail.

vii.
Griffe & Ivonbrook Granges

Climbing out of Wirksworth the walker is immediately aware of a new sense of bleakness and emptiness, in contrast to the softer landscape to the south. This is the first section of the Portway in the so-called White Peak (i.e. on limestone). There are fewer trees and farms, and settlement generally is more dispersed. Perhaps because of this, the man-made scars linked to stone quarrying and lead mining seem more obvious.

The landscape of this area between Wirksworth and Brassington was considerably altered by the construction of the Cromford and High Peak Railway in 1826, and then by the quarrying which was initially encouraged by the railway. A curious feature of this route is that it was originally planned as a canal, railways being unproven at that date, and so it was engineered in canal style, either on the level or on steep inclines (which would have been flights of locks), such as the slope leading to Middleton Top. On the 1835 map all the stations are labelled 'wharves'.

There is much debate about the likely course of the Portway just west of Wirksworth. As mentioned above, quarrying, the railway and also the construction of the Via Gellia road for Philip Gell of Hopton Hall in 1792 have all contributed to obscuring the ancient road pattern. There is a Bronze Age tumulus at Ivet Low, just south of the Brassington road, near where the builders of the Via Gellia found a Roman gravestone marking the burial place of a fifty-five year old Roman prefect called, coincidentally, 'Geli' (Cockerton, 1934d). As the Romans usually buried their dead at the roadside, this may be significant.

To the northwest the route of the Portway is much clearer. Burdett's map of 1791 shows it running directly from here to Grangemill. However, a large dusty quarry has obliterated the southern end, so to join the route it is necessary to take a footpath just past the old Hopton station, which runs northwest to Griffe Grange. This name gives a clue to the nature of the area; before the quarries the limestone hills were found ideal for grazing sheep, leading to the establishment of the large monastic farms known as granges. In the medieval period Griffe Grange belonged to Dale Abbey, to which it was directly linked by the Portway.

In pre-Roman Britain the population of this area may have been denser, judging by the wealth of prehistoric features. The most distinctive are the 'lows': Ivet Low, Minninglow, Green Low and Slipper Low are all in the locality. Confusingly, the name seems to come from the Old English *hlaw*, meaning hill or mound, often used for burial.

The section of the Portway here was known as the Chariot Way, an unlikely name which may derive from the Old English prefix cerring, a bend in a road. The bend here marked the change in direction from west to northwest. Before the Via Gellia was built this was a principal route from Derby to the northwest, and was called the old Manchester road. Today it is a broad white track, surfaced with limestone chippings, running mainly downhill from its highest point of over 300 metres. The views from here are spectacular; a farmer told me that the Wrekin is sometimes visible, over 50 miles away. The Trent valley seems much nearer, the line of the river marked by several steaming sets of cooling towers.

To the west Harborough Rocks dominate the skyline, though they look more impressive from the High Peak Trail, where the natural limestone turrets are more prominent. The name may have the same origin as Arbour Hill above Dale (see section 4 ii), as well as Arbor Low. On the northwest side of the Rocks is a cave which was inhabited when Daniel Defoe visited in 1720. He described being shown round by the woman who lived there with her leadminer husband and five children:

> ... we alighted and went in: There was a large hollow cave, which the poor people by two curtains hang'd cross, had parted into three rooms. On one side was the chimney, and the man, or perhaps his father, being miners, had found means to work a shaft or funnel through the rock to carry the smoke out at the top, where the giant's tombstone was. The habitation was poor, 'tis true, but things within did not look so like misery as I had expected. Every thing was clean and neat, tho' mean and ordinary... (Defoe, 1928 [1724] p.162).

Today the idea of living in the dripping wet cave seems incredible, although the chimney can still be seen. However, a series of excavations carried out on this site have found evidence of habitation dating back to the Bronze Age, although the latest published report (Makepeace, 2004) describes the area as an Iron Age settlement. At 379 metres the top of the Rocks offers spectacular views in all directions, from the High Peak to the north and over Carsington Water southwards. The idea of an encampment here to offer shelter to travellers is supported by the fact that another prehistoric trackway, part of which later became the Roman road to Buxton, ran west from here towards Arbor Low.

Returning to the main route, between Harborough Rocks and the Portway lies New Harboro Farm, an isolated, bleak-looking group of buildings without a single mature tree to give shelter. The view northwards is towards Winster, Elton and the indistinct hills beyond. Griffe Walk Farm is next on the left, and half a mile past this the line of the old route is blocked by the spread of Grange

Mill quarry, invisible but audible with the steady roar of heavy machines and the irritating beep of reversing trucks.

Grange Mill consists of the Holly Bush pub, an elegant furniture workshop, a farm and the old mill building, now in ruinous condition but with its large millpond surviving. The pond seems to be fed by the stream which runs down the east side of the road and presumably originates at Shothouse Spring, a constant source of water about half way up the valley. Another feature of this stretch is the outline of a possible Roman camp just north of Wigleymeadow Farm. Cockerton (1934c) suggests this might have been a half-way stage on a road between Little Chester (Derby) and Brough. Given the spring and the likely boggy nature of the valley floor it is possible that in prehistoric times the best route north was along the 300 metres contour to the east, which is achieved by taking the field path from Whitelow towards Winster.

The name Islington Lane refers to the lost village of Islington, which was a shanty town for itinerant miners. Even now it is apparent that this was lead mining country: spoil heaps and ruined buildings abound, small compounds full of weeds and junk, rusting vehicles and thistles giving a somewhat desolate feel to the landscape over a century after the industry was played out.

Harborough Rocks.

Islington Lane is unsurfaced, although in places the layer of polished stones gives it the feel of being more than a farm track. With tall hedges on both sides and frequent ash and oak trees it makes for a shady walk in summer. This section from the Winster crossroads to Robin Hood's Stride is easy to follow and is strongly suggestive of an ancient road, being part holloway. When the new turnpike (now the B5056) was constructed in the eighteenth century, the old road was cut off to force travellers onto the new route, but instead of disappearing it has survived as a green lane.

It is notable that the route runs directly between Elton and Winster, which suggests that it predated the Saxon settlement of the region, since otherwise it would have connected the villages rather than by-passing them. In fact there are no villages on the Portway between Wirksworth and Alport. Birchover and Stanton Moor dominate the landscape to the northeast, and at times the rocks of Robin Hood's Stride are visible as they become closer. The 1896 OS map shows the site of the Portaway Mine, one of the indicators of the route's existence, to the east of the junction with the Elton- Winster road. After crossing this, the route becomes surfaced and is now called Dudwood Lane. Where this rejoins the main road there is a gated track which leads up quite steeply through a meadow between the pinnacles of Robin Hood's Stride on the left and Cratcliff Rocks on the right.

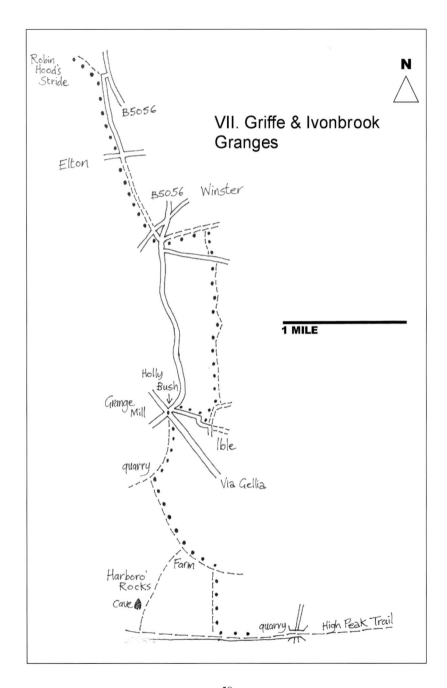

N

VII. Griffe & Ivonbrook Granges

Robin Hood's Stride

B5056

Elton

B5056 Winster

1 MILE

Holly Bush

Grange Mill

Ible

quarry

Via Gellia

Harboro' Rocks

Farm

Cave

quarry High Peak Trail

High Peak trail to Robin Hood's Stride – about 6½ miles

Continue on the High Peak Trail past the quarry to the house which must once have been the station for Hopton and Carsington. A bridleway is signposted to the right. Take this until it joins the original line of the Portway after half a mile, where you turn left. To make a detour to Harborough Rocks, take the footpath to the left at New Harboro Farm, going to the right of the farmhouse and then up the hill. The cave will be found on the far side.

Back on the main track continue for about a mile and at the T- junction by the screen of trees take the path to the right that runs down across several sloping meadows, before joining up with the old track just before Grange Mill and the Via Gellia.

At the junction cross the Via Gellia (A5012) and take the Winster road. This road is quite busy and rather narrow, making for unpleasant walking for half an hour. A more comfortable alternative is to take the right turn signposted Ible and walk uphill for half a mile to the crossroads near the deserted Whitelow Farm. Turn left here, and a hundred yards beyond the farm a path is signposted to the left. This runs for over a mile through numerous stiles to Bonsall Lane.

Turn left onto the Lane and then take the next path on the right, which leads uphill to meet the track which is now part of the Limestone Way. Turn left on this to the B5056, cross the road, and walk west for a few yards before meeting the unsurfaced Islington Lane running north. Follow this and subsequently Dudwood Lane for a mile and a half until it rejoins the B5056, where you take the stile by the gate and follow the track uphill to Robin Hood's Stride.

viii.
Robin Hood's Stride & Harthill Moor

The area around Robin Hood's Stride is known as Harthill Moor and is particularly rich in prehistoric and historic remains. Robin Hood, of course, has given his name to many landscape features in the North Midlands, and this name is probably medieval. (An alternative is Mock Beggar's Hall.) The gritstone crags would have certainly acted as a distinctive landmark for users of the Portway, and there appears to be evidence of deliberate working on them, either for quarrying or to emphasise their outline.

Among the features which are clearly man-made are the enclosure on Cratcliff Rocks, which may be late Neolithic, the circle at Nine Stone Close, which has also been given a tentative Neolithic date, at least one tumulus, and the Castle Ring hillfort. None of these can be dated accurately, and they may have been in use at different periods, e.g. the enclosure at Castle Ring to the northwest of Harthill Moor Farm might have been a replacement of the earlier stronghold on Cratcliff Rocks. Either would have provided a secure camping place for travellers. The Nine Stone circle (five of them are missing) is apparently the only one in Derbyshire with standing stones, though it has been claimed that they have been re-erected in historic times. It is noteworthy that the Nine Ladies circle is only two miles to the east on Stanton Moor.

The most recently discovered feature is an example of cup and ring art, an art form normally linked to the early Bronze Age, which was found on the base of a boulder. A possible link between these carvings and the Portway has been suggested:

> recent theories have sought to demonstrate that the siting of some prehistoric rock art may be explicable in terms of marking significant points along contemporary routes through the landscape… (Guilbert, Garton & Walters, 2006 p.20).

The same article presents a full analysis of the prehistoric features of the area.

The hermitage cave found at the west end of Cratcliff Rocks is clearly less ancient. The carved crucifix is thought to be medieval, while the records of Haddon Hall for 1550 mention paying a hermit 8d for providing rabbits (Cockerton, 1934b). What is remarkable is that this is the second hermitage on the Portway in twenty miles, and as Cockerton notes:

> it may be that the good man was able to be of assistance to travellers and performed the duties of an unofficial guide, but his choice of a hermitage can hardly have been dictated by a desire for enduring solitude (Cockerton, 1934b).

Nine Stone Circle.

Although the prominence of Robin Hood's Stride has been reduced by the planting of the belt of conifers to the south, the view from the top in all directions is still remarkable, and this would undoubtedly have been an asset to any settlement near here in earlier times. The line of ancient sweet chestnut trees on the south side of the enclosure, which marks a parish boundary, is also worth noting as this tree is uncommon in the Peak District.

VIII. Robin Hood's Stride & Harthill Moor

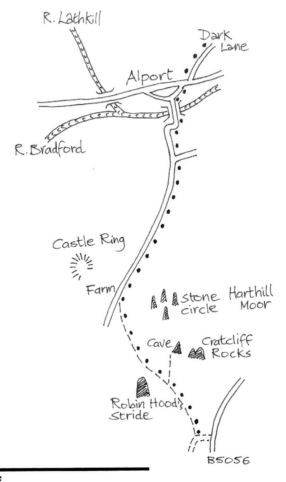

Robin Hood's Stride to Alport – about 2 miles

The path is clearly marked, with a branch leading off to the right to the Hermitage and Cratcliff Rocks. After passing Robin Hood's Stride the main path crosses two meadows before joining the Elton-Alport road, where you turn right. This quiet lane provides a comfortable stroll of just over a mile to the river crossing. Ridge and furrow fields can be seen near Upper Greenfields Farm. Then the road corkscrews for the steep descent into the pretty village of Alport, where it crosses the river just above the millpond. It is notable that by crossing here, below the point where the River Lathkill meets the Bradford, the route only needs to cross one valley and thus ford just one river, while keeping well away from the Wye valley to the east.

Harthill Hermitage.

ix.
Alport to Monsal Head

It seems hard to believe today, but according to Cockerton (1934a) in the seventeenth century the 'common highway' from Manchester to Derby and London passed over the ford at Alport, which was replaced by a bridge in 1718. This was probably a packhorse route, there being an alternative route via Buxton and Brassington. The name Alport, found both here and at Alport Height, suggests 'old Portway', perhaps a route that was already ancient when it was renamed in the early medieval period. This seems to be the only settlement which takes its name from the road, and the OS map of 1896 shows it to have been a much busier place than it is today, with a flour mill, lime kilns and smelting works.

The pattern of roads in the Haddon Fields area was significantly altered in the late eighteenth century, as explained in detail by Cockerton. Interestingly, he states that this section of the Portway remains a 'public highway', though he adds that 'its use by motor cars … is not, however, to be recommended' (Cockerton, 1934a p.21). The present condition of this stretch shows how rapidly a road can degenerate; approaching from the south there is no indication that there is even a public footpath until the barns are passed. Two hundred yards to the west of the barns lay a tumulus in which Roman coins were found, and another was sited at the junction with the Bakewell road, just visible now as a swelling in the ground next to the trig. point.

The landscape is remarkably tame compared to the region above Wirksworth: gentle slopes, few rocks and large, productive fields. Parallel to the track on the right is the well-wooded range of hills above Haddon Hall. The predominant roadside tree is the ash, characteristic of these limestone uplands, which of course is reflected in the name of the next village to be met. As was the case with previous Saxon settlements, the Portway here ignores the town of Bakewell and aims for a river crossing at Ashford.

In the first of the field paths which by-pass the town, between Haddon Fields and Crowhill Lane, it is possible to make out in the grass a raised bank running along the route. Clearly most of these small fields were enclosed in the eighteenth or nineteenth centuries, by which time the old route had become obsolete, but despite this the right of way was preserved. Consequently, this part of the route, with these footpaths going nowhere in particular, is one of the best pieces of evidence for the Portway's existence.

Crowhill Lane, which runs down the bottom of a wide, shallow valley, was not the original route to Ashford. Cockerton (1932b) points out that the four-faced marker stone at the top of the lane is labelled Buxton, Tidswell (sic), Winster and Bakewell. But today there are only three directions, which shows that the old road made directly for Ashford via a route which was largely erased when the turnpike was introduced, though the lower section still survives as John Bank Road. This joins the A6 almost opposite the lowest bridge, which may well be the site of the original ford, since the river splits into several channels here.

Ashford is a notably picturesque settlement, with three bridges over the Wye offering the watery views that always attract visitors. Only by walking this area can you appreciate how well chosen this crossing point was, since both east and west of Ashford the Wye valley has much steeper sides. The church of All Saints is probably sited near the original line of the Portway and has a lovely Romanesque tympanum showing the tree of life (presumably the ash, as in Norse mythology).

Today the direct route to Monsal Head is on the busy B6465, but there is good evidence that the Portway followed the more circular route shown on the map as Pennyunk Lane. This curious name is probably Celtic in origin; Brotherton (2005) links it to Fin Cop and believes it may have meant something like 'headland of the youth'. Penn means hilltop (Pennine may have the same root), and the lane passes just below the ten-acre site of Fin Cop, which overlooks the slopes of Monsal Dale. It is often described as an Iron Age hillfort, but there is much uncertainty about this. It was clearly a defensive site, protected partly by earth ramparts and partly by the steep drop into the Wye valley, but its purpose is unknown and Bronze Age burials as well as Neolithic remains have been found within. It may well have had different functions in different periods, and could certainly have sheltered Portway travellers.

Although parts of Pennyunk Lane would have been realigned when the land was enclosed and the stone walls built, it seems likely that this was the original route that led to Fin Cop, as well as being the main road north. The lane is now a pretty, tranquil walk, lined with low stone walls and the upland pastures of grazing cows. It is also well above the course of the main road, offering spectacular views to the north, east and south, while as you approach Monsal the pointed summit of Wardlow Hay Cop (370 metres) provides a useful marker. When the viewpoint at Monsal Head is reached it is clear that the route that has been followed (i.e. crossing the Wye at Ashford) is far easier than if the crossing had been made further upstream, where the river runs in a much deeper valley.

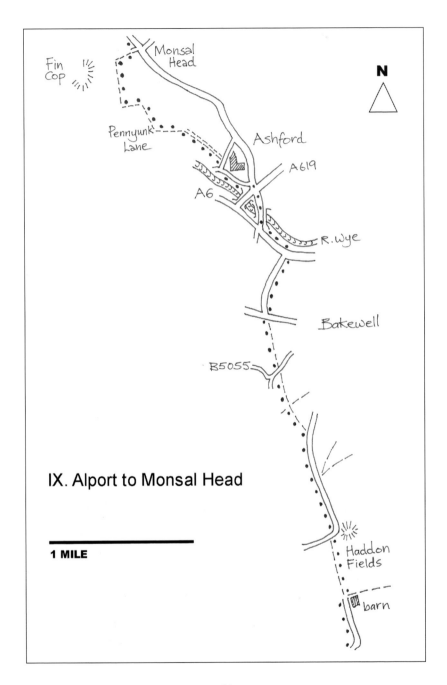

Fin Cop

Monsal Head

Pennyunk Lane

Ashford

A619

A6

R. Wye

Bakewell

B5055

IX. Alport to Monsal Head

1 MILE

Haddon Fields

barn

N

Alport to Monsal Head – about 5 miles

On the other side of the Youlgreave road take Dark Lane to climb steeply out of the valley and on to the plateau of Haddon Fields above. On reaching the straggling barns at the end of the road there is no clue that there are three public footpaths beyond this point. The line of the Portway is straight ahead, almost due north, to the east of the wall until you join the road at a bend near a trig. point at 208 metres.

The route now runs downhill on the road for just under a mile before a footpath is marked on the left. Take the path, which runs first down to a stile, then across a narrow field and then up through several more fields. After crossing the busy Monyash-Bakewell road the path becomes more tortuous as it wanders through a maze of small walled fields with numerous stiles, finally emerging on the road just before Crowhill Lane. The old marker stone can be found at the head of this lane, which gives a gentle descent to the Wye valley and the A6. This must be followed to the west for less than half a mile to Ashford, but fortunately a pavement means there is no need to walk on the road.

Cross the river by the first bridge and then cross the A6020 into Church Street. Walk past the church and turn right up Fennel Street. Either take the path signed to the left or continue to the top where there is a track running northwest at Highfields. Both lead into Pennyunk Lane, which changes from a track to a fieldpath before reaching the vicinity of Fin Cop. As it approaches the hamlet of Monsal Head the original line of the route is lost and the path emerges from the bushes directly above the railway viaduct.

Ashford Church tympanum.

67

X.
Tideslow & Mam Tor

Monsal Head provides a good view of the Fin Cop site to the west, making full use of the defensive position provided by the bend in the river. At the same time it can be seen how well the line of the Portway avoids the steep valleys in this area by keeping to the plateau to the east. The road north from here to Wardlow Mires is called Castlegate; the identity of the castle to which it led is unclear, but the route gives splendid views both east and west. The first two miles go steadily uphill, reaching a summit near Rolley Low on the left, the second burial mound on this stretch. On the other side of the road, under a hawthorn tree, is an old milestone with a benchmark cut into it but otherwise too worn to read.

The next stage runs downhill through the strung-out village of Wardlow. One feature of this area is the tiny walled fields on both sides of the road, which must reflect the complexity of land divisions at enclosure. Tideslow becomes a more prominent landmark to the northwest as you drop down. Wardlow Mires is surely one of the less attractive place names in Derbyshire, and the reality lives up to it.

The problem of the line of the Portway at Wardlow Mires is dealt with in some detail by Cockerton (1932d). Briefly, he showed that the building of the turnpike not only obliterated this section, but also destroyed a sizeable barrow called Stoney Low which had existed here beside the line of the road. However, the lower part of Trot Lane, just north of the A623, is in alignment with the old route, and at the junction of Trot Lane with the track up to Stanley House, looking west, a very substantial holloway can be seen in the field leading directly towards Tideslow. This is one of those points where the reality of the ancient route appears conclusive, so clear is the evidence on the ground.

On the map it can be seen that this line continues as both field boundaries and the parish boundary to the Little Hucklow road, after which it becomes lost in the very regular enclosure pattern of fields around Rising Sun Farm. The same line can be seen, looking back, from the top of Tideslow. This must have been the last significant landmark before Mam Tor, which is clearly visible as you approach, ascending Tideswell Rake. The whole summit of this low has been extensively disturbed, which obscures the fact that it was one of the largest Neolithic round barrows in the county (Radley & Plant, 1971). It appears to have been plundered first by lead miners and then dug by Victorian archaeologists, so that establishing its history is even more challenging than usual.

The route of the last stage of the Portway, from Tideslow to Mam Tor, has never been established, though the most obvious line runs north from Tideslow on a clear track. Although this is the easiest and possibly the most pleasant route, it has the drawback of not passing the site of the Portway Mine, which lies a few hundred yards to the west. The original and more circuitous route probably avoided the highest point of Bradwell Moor by looping round this to the west at the Cop, and then curving round the head of Conies Dale to join the other track near Oxlow House. A significant part of this route is a parish boundary, and although one section is not a footpath, it is on access land. The name Cop, reminiscent of nearby Fin Cop, seems to suggest a distinct headland, as can be seen from a distance above the farm.

The alternative route, which is easier to navigate in poor weather, runs first between meadows, then passes through a narrow belt of trees before meeting Batham Gate, the Roman road from Buxton to Brough. Looking south from here it can be seen that Tideslow was an effective landmark long before the mast was erected. Cockerton (1933a) explained that the kink in the line of Batham Gate at this point shows that the Portway was in existence before the Romans arrived.

The route then crosses moorland, running downhill to meet a track below Rowter Farm, the only settlement on this section. Beyond the farm Mam Tor, with its scar of landslip to the southeast face, becomes clearly visible, and soon the double horseshoe of ramparts can be made out. Crossing two roads, the track runs directly to Mam Gap, from where there is a clear paved path to the summit.

Given its prominent site and importance as the largest of Derbyshire's hillforts, as well as the excavation work that has been carried out here, it is surprising how little is known of Mam Tor. The name is thought to be Celtic, meaning breast, though perhaps the shape of the hill has changed over the millennia (it is also called the Shivering Mountain). There appears to have been either permanent or temporary settlement here, judging by the many hut bases that have been discovered. Yet even if the climate was warmer, it is hard to imagine year-round settlement at over 500 metres. It has been suggested that the huts were for occupation in periods of conflict, or possibly by summer pastoralists, but they could equally have accommodated pilgrims during seasonal festivals. These hut sites, which may have been in use from 1100 BC, as well as two Bronze Age barrows, seem to predate the ramparts, which appear to belong to the Iron Age.

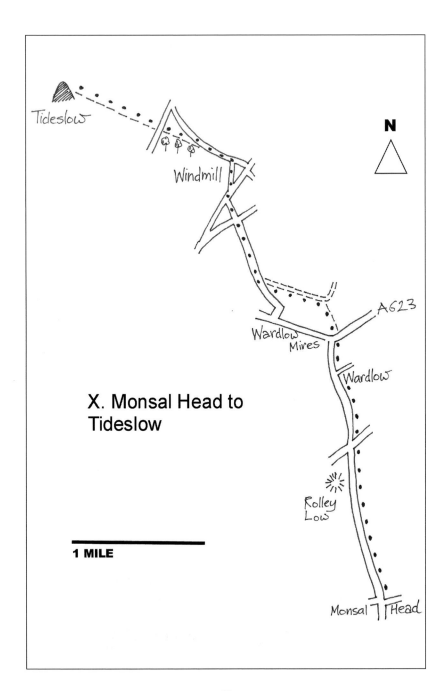

Tideslow

Windmill

N

A623

Wardlow Mires

Wardlow

X. Monsal Head to Tideslow

Rolley Low

1 MILE

Monsal Head

Monsal Head to Mam Tor – about 10 miles
by more direct route

The next three miles have to be walked on a fairly busy road, but the views are some compensation for this. (The alternative is to drop down from Monsal Head to the track through Cressbrook Dale.) Castlegate runs nearly due north, uphill, for over a mile and a half to the crossroads with the road to Foolow. After this there is a pavement for the rest of the way through Wardlow to the junction with the busy A623.

The next stage cannot be walked on the line of the Portway, as no rights of way exist. The suggested route follows it quite closely, but clearly other options are possible. Turn right at the T- junction, past the Three Stags pub and take the footpath signed to the left. Follow the signs through the farmyard and then uphill towards Stanley House. Climb the stile here and join a narrow road west. This leads to a junction with Trot Lane, where the line of the Portway in a holloway can be seen from the field gate opposite. Take Trot Lane uphill to the junction with the B6049, turn right and go up to the hamlet of Windmill. From here a minor road runs uphill to the west, and just after leaving the houses you see the traces of a mining rake, here known as High Rake. Take the track which forks off to the left along the rake. Soon you pass the excavations of High Rake mine. The path crosses a road, and then you have to keep to the left hand wall. The ground is heavily disturbed all the way up and all over the top of Tideslow, from where there are excellent views back to Wardlow Mires.

Mam Tor and Rowter Farm.

X. Tideslow to Mam Tor

N

Mam Tor

Castleton

B6061

Rowter Farm

← no path

Portway Mine site

The Cop

Cop Round

farm

Tideslow

... direct route

1 MILE

Probable original route

From the top of Tideslow continue west until you reach a minor road. Cross this, and take the next path across five fields before coming out on Pittlesmere Lane. Follow this for a short distance before finding a path marked to the north. This field path avoids the higher ground to the east and crosses the line of Batham Gate, which is quite invisible on the ground. After crossing another minor road the path runs mainly downhill to join the road that leads up to Cop Farm. This is designated as the Limestone Way. Walk past and to the right of the farm and join a narrow walled lane, called Dick Lane on the OS map of 1896. Follow this up to the summit (Cop Round) and down the other side to where the track crosses Oxlow Rake, a distinctive area of mining disturbance. Now follow the curve of the wall over the moor to the northwest until eventually meeting up with the footpath coming from near Oxlow House. Here you cross the B6061 and then you soon reach the Chapel-en-le-Frith road. Beyond this is the base of Mam Tor, and by climbing up to Mam Gap you will find the paved path to the top.

Simpler and more direct route

The logical way from the top of Tideslow would be to go due north to join the clearly visible track leading to Mam Tor, but as there is no right of way it is necessary to go west to the road and then back via Bushey Heath Farm to link up with this route. Take the track to the east of Bushey Heath Farm until it meets the road. Follow the road north for a short distance until it bends to the east, then take the track north. This soon becomes an unfenced path on moorland and eventually runs downhill to a junction of five ways. Go through the gate to the left, and after a hundred yards bear right towards Rowter Farm. This section runs over the hill and down to the B6061. Cross this and follow the directions above.

Tideslow from Trot Lane.

Appendix 1

**Articles by R.W.P. Cockerton in *Derbyshire Countryside*
related to the Portway.**

Vol. 2 1932

January (5)   Preliminary note (1932a)

April (6)   Derbygate (1932b)

July (7)   Castlegate (1932c)

October (8)   Castlegate continued (1932d)

Vol. 3 1933

July (11)   Meaning of the name (1933a)

October (12)   Meaning of the name continued (1933b)

Vol. 4 1934

January (13)   Haddon Fields (1934a)

April (14)   Harthill Moor (1934b)

July (15)   Ivonbrook Grange (1934c)

October (16)   Chariot Way (1934d)

Vol. 5 1935

January (17)   Sandiacre (1935a)

April (18)   Dale Abbey (1935b)

October (20)   Stanley (1935c)

Vol. 6 1936

January (21)   Coxbench (1936a)

July (23)   Wirksworth (1936b)

Appendix 2

Some prehistoric and historic features on the presumed line of the Portway.

Place	Feature
Stapleford Hill	Hemlock Stone
Stapleford churchyard	Cross
Sandiacre	St Giles church
Ladycross Lane	*Cross*
Dale	Hermitage
Dale	Church & *Abbey*
Dale – Arbour Hill	Encampment
Morley	St Mathew's church
Morley churchyard	Crosses
Morley	Moated mound
Horsley Castle	Castle
Coxbench	Mound/ tumulus
Coxbench	St Anthony's Well
Holbrook Hall grounds	Roman kilns
Alport Height	Landmark
Wirksworth east	Standing stone opposite Malt Shovel Inn
Wirksworth	St Mary's church
Wirksworth west	Standing stone above Norbreck Farm
Wirksworth west	Ivet Low/ tumulus
Harborough Rocks	Encampment
Robin Hood's Stride	Landmark
Cratcliff Rocks	Hermitage & encampment
Harthill Moor	Stone circle/rock art

Castle Ring	Encampment
Haddon Fields	Tumulus
Ashford	Holy Trinity church
Fin Cop	Encampment
Rolley Low	Tumulus
Wardlow Mires	*Tumulus (Stoney Low)*
Tideslow	Landmark/*Tumulus*
The Cop	Landmark
Mam Tor	Landmark/ Encampment

N.B. Many features have been lost due to ploughing or quarrying.
Italics denotes that this feature is lost, though documented.

References & Bibliography

Abbreviation: DAJ – *Derbyshire Archaeological Journal*

Bevan, B. (2004) *The Upper Derwent: 10,000 Years in a Peak District Valley*. Stroud: Tempus

Brotherton, P. (2005) *Celtic Place Names and Archaeology in Derbyshire*. DAJ 125, 100-137

Burdett, P. (1767/ 1791) *Map of Derbyshire*

Cameron, K. (1959) *The Place Names of Derbyshire*. Cambridge: Cambridge University Press

Cockerton, R.W.P. *See Appendix 1*

Cohen, E. (1992) 'Pilgrimage and Tourism: Convergence and Divergence' in Morinis, A. (ed.), *Sacred Journeys*. Westport: Greenwood Press

Cotton, C. (1681) *The Wonders of the Peak*. London: Brome

Davies, D. (1811) *History of Derbyshire*. Belper: Mason

Defoe, D. (1928 [1724]) *A Tour of England & Wales*. London: Dent

Dodd A.E. & Dodd E.M. (1980) *Peakland Roads and Trackways*. Moorland

Elsner, J. & Rutherford, I. (eds) (2005) *Pilgrimage in Graeco-Roman & Early Christian Antiquity*. Oxford: Oxford University Press

Guilbert, G., Garton, D. & Walters, D. (2006) *Prehistoric Cup-and-Ring Art at the Heart of Harthill Moor*. DAJ 126, 12-30

Hallenday, N. (2001) *Inuksuit: Silent Messengers of the Arctic*. Washington: University of Washington Press

Hodges, R. (1991) *Wall-to Wall History, The Story of Roystone Grange*. London: Duckworth

Howe, D. (1984) *The Story of Holbrook*. Cromford: Scarthin

Hutton, R. (1996) *The Stations of the Sun*. Oxford: Oxford University Press

Makepeace, G. (2004) *Harborough Rocks – Early Iron Age Settlement, Near Brassington, Derbyshire*. DAJ 124, 64-68

Morley Village History Committee (1977) *History of the Parish of Morley*

Ordnance Survey (1896) *Map of Derbyshire 1:2500*

Palfreyman, A. (2001) *Report on the Excavation of a Romano-British Aisled Building at Little Hay Grange Farm, Ockbrook, Derbyshire 1994-97*. DAJ 121

Palfreyman, A. & Ebbins, S. (2007) *A Romano-British Quern-Manufacturing Site at Blackbrook, Derbyshire*. DAJ 127, 33-48

Pevsner, N. (1978) Derbyshire (The Buildings of England). Harmondsworth: Penguin

Preston, J. (1992) 'Spiritual Magnetism: An Organizing Principle for the Study of Pilgrimage', in Morinis, A. (ed.), *Sacred Journeys*. Westport: Greenwood Press

Radley, J., & Plant, M. (1971) *Tideslow: a Neolithic Round Barrow at Tideswell*. DAJ 91

Sanderson, G. (1835) *Map: Twenty Miles Around Mansfield*

Shone, A. (unpublished) *Origins & History of Wirksworth*

Spencer, C. (1993) *Walking the Derbyshire Portway*. Hillsboro

Stone, R. (2005) *The River Trent*. Chichester: Phillimore

Taylor, C. (1979) *Roads & Tracks of Britain*. London: Dent

Turbutt, G. (2007) *Unresolved Mysteries of Derbyshire History*. DAJ 127, 1-14

Ward, J. (1891) *Dale and its Abbey, Derbyshire*. Derby: Frank Murray

Watson, W. (1986) *The Illustrated History of Duffield*. Duffield: Chevin Books